T0380863

Maine Wildflowers

in Vision and Verse

Jean Edwards

To order additional copies of this book, contact:
Xlibris
1-888-795-4274
www.Xlibris.com
Orders@Xlibris.com

ISBN: Softcover   978-1-4535-7512-3
        Hardcover   978-1-4535-7513-0
        EBook   978-1-7960-7784-1

Print information available on the last page

Rev. date: 12/11/2019

Contents

Posies

Lupines and daisies
Buttercups and fence rose,
Paint brushes and honeysuckle vines,
Gentian and crown vetch
Yarrow and clover,
Bluets and Queen Anne so fine.

Pink slippers and cat's paws
Tiger lilies and pulpits
Trillium and plantain sublime,
Poppies and violets
Snap dragon's and Quakers,
These will I save in my mind.

Lupines

If I could choose the perfect time of year to journey East,

I'd want to travel in mid-June and let my vision feast

On those amazing fields of color, purple, pink and blue,

That cover fields and roadsides and hills within my view.

I think perhaps the story that they tell so well must be,

That we should flourish for awhile, and live lives brilliantly,

And then before we fade away when we have done our best

To plant our seeds, we shed our blooms like lupines,

And lay us down to rest.

Jack in the Pulpit

Preacher, preacher in the wood, why so somber 'neath your hood

Of gentle green and darker hue that shades you from a stranger's view?

Do you have words of wisdom rare, that you could with a wanderer share?

Here in your dark and damp domain your solemn purple suit remains

A pleasant sober joy for me to view your calm simplicity.

Perhaps the message that you give is that we should more simply live,

Forgetting all the rush of life, foregoing worry, fuss and strife.

Here, sheltered from the world, I find, your lesson brings me peace of mind.

Quaker Ladies

Quaker Ladies in your snowy huddle, dancing in the gentle springtime breeze,

Embracing one another as you cuddle, as loving sisters you attempt to please.

Do you remain in groups because you're shy, or do you seek to ward off evening chill?

You turn your tiny faces to the sky until the evening bids the breeze, "be still."

Like patches of a sudden springtime snow, that unexpectedly decides to fall,

Your fragile groups appear, a sudden show of bluish white that brings a thrill to all.

Briefly, you arrive in early spring, to touch our hearts with beauty that you bring.

Socrates

So you thought it was the hemlock tree that poisoned poor old Socrates.

For him a deadly plant was found, whose roots and stems were finely ground,

And added to a liquid, poured into his ears as soundly snored,

The unsuspecting Senator and ended life for the orator.

His wisdom lives but in that hour his life was quenched by a white wild flower.

So never place your sacred trust in looks alone, but if you must,

Find beauty that you can embrace, place fair of soul above fair of face.

Ode to the Cabbage

There are cabbages red and cabbages white and flowering cabbage for show,

But of all the cabbages, one stands alone, and has more attributes than you know.

Synplocarpus foetious is the most potent you'll find, its aroma most powerful of all.

It blooms by the streams and wet river banks, and flourishes spring, summer and fall.

Perhaps you have seen it and thought its lone job, was to manufacture its smell.

Now we find it breeds bugs, both mosquitoes and flies in its

purplish spathe center as well.

Now we admire the spring green that we find, and the sweet

smelling buds in the bowers,

But beware of the cabbage named after the skunk, don't mistake it

for pluckable flowers!

Blossom

Across the field where brook doth flow, beyond the hill where berries grow,

On past the hedge of snake bush there, be sure you walk with extra care,

Lest there beneath your foot you find a blossom of another kind.

You may retrace steps of bovine that sauntered there another time.

Don't crush a fragrant pasture bloom or cow blossom angst will be your doom.

Of all the flowers I have found, the cow blossom fragrance most profound.

Cattails

If I were a Cattail, here's what I'd do, I'd find many ways to make life easy for you.

My blooms are not strictly my plant to adorn, just pluck them

and boil them like small ears of corn.

You'd find them quite tasty when eaten at dinner, when buttered

this veggie becomes a lunch winner.

And then I would give you my tough lengthy leaves, so handy

and helpful when baskets you weave.

Just harvest my roots like potatoes, for baking, or steaming and

peeling for eating, or making

A salad with dressing and onions and things, for picnics or

dinner or celebratory flings.

When my seed pods ripen and turn to soft fluffing,

You'll find it is perfect for small pillow stuffing.

By peeling my roots and grinding them fine into flour for using at some future time,

A cake or some biscuits you could easily cook, and who

would surmise from the baked goods look,

That they came from a plant that in water had grown,

for most of my uses are largely unknown.

So eat hearty, weave wisely, with never a fear, by roadside

and stream edge, I'll be waiting here.

Black Eyed Susan

What is that yellow and brown I see, yonder dark eyes smiling at me?

Brightening roadsides, edging the fields, glowing with color that warm July yields,

Waving a greeting to catch my eye, brilliantly nodding as I pass on by.

Susan with dark eyes and tresses of gold, the most joyful a picture

that one could behold.

Flower Seasons

Who will be first, said the returning sun.
"Who wants to bloom first, when winter is done?
The crocus spoke up, "The first will be me, my blossom's
the first springtime flower you'll see,
While the snow still lingers I'll push my blooms through
the snow with my blossoms of white, yellow and blue."
"I will be next," the mayflower said. "Deep in the woods I'll raise my pink head.
My perfume will be sweetly enchanting the spring.
Being second is fine, when such pleasure I bring."
"I'm third," said the violet, "My green leaves are new, and
my small fragrant blossoms are indigo blue."
Then, small Quaker Ladies, their chorus rang out,
"We're here on the hill where the dandelions sprout.
We're waiting for lilacs and blossoms on trees,
We're ready with nectar for striped honey bees."
Soon lupines will open on roadsides and fields,
and daisies and buttercups add to the yield,
Of colorful blooms that pleasure the eyes under soft
fluffy clouds 'neath blue summer skies,
Until finally asters and bright goldenrod are scattered
about near gray milkweed pods.
Perhaps there's no hurry, there's time for them all to greet
the warm sunshine, from spring until fall.

Spring to Autumn

Alexandra gold and apple blossom white, what is this glorious display

That falls within my sight? The one will someday be a fruit,

The other just a weed. One satisfies our hunger, one feeds a soul in need.

And when the harvest's gathered in, and fruit is opened wide,

The white of apple blossoms will show itself inside.

The golden Alexandra will then be past its bloom,

But goldenrod will take its place in fields where there is room

To grow and flourish brightly by every stone piled wall,

And springtime colors carry on, to cheer us through the fall.

Weeds

Eating weeds seems strange to me, while for some a natural act,

Most veggie treats are planted in a garden, that's a fact.

A regular potato, a tomato, red and round,

May be grown in plots and raised beds, while weeds are easily found,

Most anywhere that there is dirt, and by gardeners detested,

Lest they crowd out cultivated plants, so their growth must be arrested.

The dandelion likes to sprout in every open field,

It makes a dandy salad or a veggie at your meal.

The yellow flowered mustard may be wretched weeds to some,

But cook some up with ham hocks if you like your greens well done.

Now there's the plantain by the path, arriving on the scene,

More "A" and "C" than spinach, a most edible wild green.

And dock may be ugly but take extra care, it is a great food, you should be aware.

The brown fruits of the plant, the Indians found,

Made a great flour for baking when they're finely ground.

And then the burdock that you thought was an aggravating weed,

It's root, when boiled is tasty, when you saw only that its seed,

Was a sticky, pesky, tangler that was hateful to your hair,

Never knowing that its stems, when peeled, will with asparagus compare.

So step carefully and don't distain a weed you do not know.

That weed could be salvation, if your garden fails to grow.

Shall We Dance?

"Shall we dance?" said the wildflowers, as they were swaying to and fro.

"Shall we cavort on this joyous day as pleasant breezes blow?

Our lives are very short, so we must always take,

Each opportunity we find, to dance and celebrate.

The springtime breeze and happy showers splashing on the ground,

Morning sunrise, floating clouds, shadow patterns we have found.

Don't take us for granted, we will not linger long,

When autumn comes we will return to earth where we belong.

Our seeds will fall and take their rest 'til springtime comes again,

Then we will sprout and rise again, in warming April rain.

Don't pass us by, take time to join our waltz beneath the sun,

Let's dance through days of summer, until our season's done."

Buttercup

Some springs are golden yellow as the fields burst into bloom,
Crowding every hillside, anywhere there's room,
To grow their slender, leafless stems that glow in morning sun,
And nod their sunny faces in evening breeze, when day is done.

Quaker Ladies II

We gather on the hilltop before the break of day,

And tilt our faces to the east when sunshine's on the way.

We nod in group agreement, our white bonnets shade our eyes,

From springtime sun that glows beneath the blue of springtime skies.

We brought our sewing baskets, we brought our noontime lunch,

We are a sisterhood of joy, a dedicated bunch.

We'll sew our quilts and samplers, we'll eat our lunch and pray.

We're reverent Quaker Ladies with much to do today.

Ferns

How many different kinds of ferns will grow

When springtime bursts its bonds?

And all along the forest edge

We see the lacy fronds.

There by the rock wall, fiddle heads

Present their curling stems,

And clusters of another kind

Are huddled there to lend,

A woven backdrop for some flower,

Much in need of shade's

Protection by the bower.

And every one is special

While yet they're much the same,

I find their varying beauty deserves

A much more royal name.

Fiddle

Play, fiddle, play,

Play a happy tune today,

Song of cheer from singing sparrow,

Breeze that whispers through the yarrow.

Joyfully caress the earth,

Melodies of nature's mirth.

Fiddle, play, as daisies dance,

Buzzing sound of bee romance,

As flower to flower the pollen spreads

From every bud and flower bed.

Tender chirping newborn sound,

Raindrops splashing on the ground,

Fiddle, work your charm for me,

Play your summer harmony,

Let me hear your melody.

Play, fiddle, play.

Cookies

My mother tried to kill me, when I was just a child

At least that's what I thought in later years.

Perhaps it's only that she trusted me and thought me very bright,

And so that error had controlled her fears.

"I'll make some cookies," she had said, "If help me some, you will,

Go gather caraway for me,"(not knowing herbs can kill.)

And so I ventured forth, you see, with bucket in my hand,

To gather seeds for flavoring from near-by roadside land.

She didn't know, I later thought, that also growing wild

That dreaded killer, hemlock grew, (for I was just a child).

So happily I filled my pail and hurried home again,

Not dreaming I might gather seed that could cause someone pain.

I know I ate those cookies, and lived to tell the tale,

So perhaps it was real caraway I gathered in the pail.

My mother never knew the doubts I held in later years.

I had survived the cookies and she never knew my fears.

Little did I realize that she had carefully,

Examined all the seeds I brought, before baking them for me.

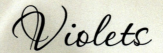 Violets

On a cool September morning when the air was crisp and still

I asked myself what project should I attempt, my day to fill.

I wandered to the attic, to take a look around

And there among the dusty broken chairs and frames I found

A wooden, banded trunk, with brass corners on the frame.

It was my Grandpa's old sea trunk,

And on top was carved his name.

I wondered what I'd find within this relic stored away,

And what I found has changed the way I think and feel today.

There was a small tea service of thinnest porcelain,

There was a rolled up scarf that I unfurled, of softest silk, I stroked its folds

When out fell a wrinkled photograph of a smiling Asian girl.

I wondered who the person was, she wasn't my Grandma.

With a sudden jolt I realized, it was a friend of my Grandpa.

A stack of letters tied in blue were there beneath some things,

Old uniforms, a sailor hat, a small tin filled with rings.

Another picture in a frame that was a visage clear,

A young sailor, my grandfather, with a gold ring in his ear.

It struck me then, that years had changed a young man over time,

For the sailor in the picture was that old grandpa of mine.

At the bottom of the trunk I found a Bible, leather bound.

A precious relic from the past among the treasure trove I'd found.

With care, I let it open to a place the pages fell

And knew the violets pressed there would now their story tell.

I was drawn back to the letters, in ribbon neatly tied,

They would reveal the secrets that might be stored inside.

"My Darling Genevieve," it said. "Tonight we will set sail,

It's been a long time for us both. I confess I nearly failed

Our vows. I was so very lonesome and I met a lovely girl.

I thought perhaps I'd stay here in this far off foreign world.

The violets you sent me have turned my heart around.

My home in Maine and thoughts of you now head me homeward bound.

Now we are ready to depart and I'll be coming home.

I'm giving up this sailor's life and my heart will never roam.

I realize that you, dear one, are the true love of my life,

I vow to love you always, my love, my heart, my wife."

I carefully replaced the letter that was yellowed by the years

And closed the trunk and latched it, and smiling through my tears,

I thought about my Grandpa. Once he was young and wild,

But he became a loving man, and I, his adoring grandchild.

Blueberries

Those waxy blossoms cuddle there, among their shiny leaves,

So suddenly they all appear to make a soul believe

There is a God, for surely such wonder cannot be

An accident of nature, these fields of blooms we see.

And think about the harvest that an August sun will yield,

When small white blooms will turn to blue in every fruited field.

The Barrens

August sun is rising and burning off the dew,

I hear the barrens calling, "Come to fields of berry blue."

Answering the call, I stroll familiar berry fields,

Now ready for the harvest, the rising mist reveals.

I smell the pungent fragrance that only here is found,

Rising with each step I take upon the fruitful ground.

I see, I smell, I touch, with feeling ever new,

Filling me with wonder like no other place can do.

And when my life is over, let me rest near land I knew,

And I can rest forever, near fields of berry blue.

The Lilac Tree

"Meet me by the lilacs growing by the river bend,

You can always count on me, my love will never end.

I'll wait for you, I promise, if you're late I'll still be there,

Waiting by the lilac tree, so meet me if you care."

I remember that request you made so very long ago,

It's sweetly etched upon my heart more dearly than you know.

I met you and together we made our two lives one,

The lilac tree was where we met and where our marriage was begun.

Our wedding was so happy because we chose this special place,

To bind our hearts together, heart to heart and face to face.

We held each other's hands that day, exchanging vows and rings,

Never dreaming there would come a day we'd part for anything.

But then they sent you far away, away across the sea,

And you were taken from this earth, and taken, too, from me.

The lilac blooms have gone away, the time of blossoming is past,

And now the long awaited day has come to me, at last.

They brought you to your home again, you have come back to me,

And so you rest where we loved best, beneath the lilac tree.

Dandelion

Winter snow has disappeared and warming winds prevail,

The greening of the earth a welcome sight,

But then among awaited flowers,

The anxious plant arrives that sprouted overnight.

You may despise the lowly weed and wish its growth abate,

But think again before you judge, and leave the plant to fate.

The pilgrims did survive on such an edible green weed,

It saved them from much sickness in their desperate time of need.

A dandelion salad, or dandelion greens,

A rare gourmet perfection providing vitamins, it seems.

A dash of apple vinegar, some butter, freshly churned,

Give the lowly dandelion the respect that it has earned.

The honeybees find nectar in the golden yellow blooms,

And dandelion wine, of course, can chase away the gloom.

Some may not like the greens to eat or appreciate the wine,

The weed may not a smooth lawn make, and that is all just fine,

But when they grow too tough to eat the yellow blossoms fade at night,

And the field is covered over with snowy puffs of white,

If you will wait, the day will come when breezes start to blow,

And on that breeze the gentle seeds float by like flakes of snow.

Strawberries

I   hope the Boston folk were pleased with the fruit I gathered on my knees,

As spying flowers in the spring and knowing of the fruit it brings,

I hesitate in my admiration and offer you this admonition.

The innocence of that small bloom may bring joy to your heart

But hard work will result from that innocent start.

The luscious fruit that you enjoy deserves respect and appreciation.

Not easy is the gathering of that strawberry sensation.

"Here are your baskets," said the man, "Fill them as fully as you can.

Three cents a basket you'll earn for each one,"

So fill them I did 'til the long day was done.

I hadn't bargained for the ache or how much effort it would take

To earn my clothes for the school year to start

So I began to pick with a happy heart. Soon came fatigue of the vertebrae,

And I could perceive a long miserable day.

So dropping to my knees I quickly was found to be crawling

along on rough stubble ground.

"Stay in your row," the boss advised, when larger fruit across I spied.

In the heat of the sun my endurance was slipping, but I continued

to pick the fruit for shipping.

I wonder now, "Was it really that bad?" Perhaps not, but it was the only job I had,

So I worked through the season and earned my school clothes,

and who in Boston ate those berries, nobody knows.

Forget Me Not

She said "Please don't forget me, when I have gone away.

Remember all the good times that we had,

When we were all together, and the fun tricks that we played upon

each other and the laughter that we shared.

Each moment was so precious, I enjoyed them, every one,

and I'm sorry that I had to leave, you see.

But carry on your lives, just as you did before, and when

you get together, will you please remember me."

When I think of all the people who say "forget me not," the one I think of most is always you. You never voiced a sad complaint, though you knew the end was near, and so your sweet "forget me not" is the one I hold most dear.

I can't forget pale tumbling curls or smiling eyes of blue.

I can't forget the joys we shared together, me and you.

Then there were days of laughter after all the pranks we played, happy get-togethers and all the meals we made.

You had a happy spirit, you had love for all you knew,

I see you in the flowers, forget me nots of blue.

Wildflowers

If all the world would just observe

The flowers of the field,

They always seem to complement each other.

They share all this earth offers them

In every kind of weather,

Accepting different colors,

Different shapes and different ways.

They bloom at different times of year,

Offering beautiful displays.

We humans seem to find much fault

With those who don't conform,

And criticize, berate, neglect

Those who were different born.

Why can't we learn a lesson

And our prejudices yield,

And learn to love our brothers

Like the flowers of the field.

Printed in the United States
By Bookmasters